The Little Book of Autism FAQs

How to Talk with Your Child about their Diagnosis
& Other Conversations

Davida Hartman

Illustrated by **Margaret Anne Suggs**

Jessica Kingsley *Publishers*
London and Philadelphia

First published in 2020
by Jessica Kingsley Publishers
73 Collier Street
London N1 9BE, UK
and
400 Market Street, Suite 400
Philadelphia, PA 19106, USA

www.jkp.com

Library of Congress Cataloging in Publication Data
A CIP catalog record for this book is available from the Library of Congress

British Library Cataloguing in Publication Data
A CIP catalogue record for this book is available from the British Library

ISBN 978 1 78592 449 1
eISBN 978 1 78450 824 1

Printed and bound in Great Britain

Dedication

So many autistic children, teenagers and adults generously gave their time and energy to this book. It is dedicated to them, in the hope that it not only helps them and others like them, but also that it contributes to a wider conversation about autism awareness, understanding and acceptance and ultimately helps build safer, kinder and more inclusive communities for all.

Contents

I have pride and confidence in my autism
because I had parents who are open.

(Ben, aged 16)

You don't look autistic isn't a compliment to me.
It means that people don't understand autism and
still think it looks a certain way. It makes me feel
like I don't belong in the autistic community.

(Still Living @TeenAspie, 10.29pm, 29 October 2018)

Introduction

For parents of children newly diagnosed with autism, wondering *if*, or *just how*, they are going to tell their child is a huge area of concern, and the stress of 'getting it right' can often delay any conversations even starting.

So, let's start by doing away with the concept of 'getting it right' altogether. Parenting is not an exact science. You probably *will* say the wrong thing at some stage, because you are *human*. But remember this: more important than any of the individual words you use to try to explain a difficult concept, such as autism, is that your child knows that you love and accept them for *everything* they are (including the autism). Everything else is just icing on the cake.

Also, remember that autism is a complicated topic. No matter how verbal or able they are, your child is not going to understand everything about it the first time you talk to them about it. And that is OK. To expect them to would not only be unrealistic but actually impossible. So don't put too much pressure on yourself either to know everything about autism or explain it all really well during those early conversations. Your child's understanding of autism, like yours, will grow over time and with lived experience of how autism affects them and you specifically.

I have included in this book all of the most common questions that parents ask me post diagnosis in this area, and my typical responses to them. To help you get going, I have included some examples of ways you can talk about autism with your child.

I have included some recommended books, videos, movies, documentaries and activities. I have also included Q&As from autistic children and adults, so that you can hear how they feel about this subject, in their own words.

My hope in writing this book is that it gives you the confidence to get those autism conversations started with your children, in all their glorious and loving imperfection. Because, in my experience, the difference in your child's life if you do will be immeasurable.

Important note

It is important to acknowledge that, while there are recommendations included in this book for children with minimal verbal language and an additional intellectual disability, it is mostly geared towards autistic children with basic language skills.

CHAPTER 1

What Is Autism Anyway?

Q&A BRIAN, AGED 28

1. What age were you when you found out about your autism diagnosis?

I was almost 22 when I found out about my diagnosis. It was recommended I investigate an autism diagnosis after an original diagnosis of dysgraphia, a year prior.

2. How did you find out?

Since I was diagnosed with dysgraphia while I was preparing to retake my final year exams at school, my parents, assessor and teachers decided it might be best to leave me to get used to dysgraphia before I investigated autism. I chose to pursue an assessment for autism and was diagnosed at my home by a clinical psychologist.

3. How did you feel about it when you did find out?

I was immensely relieved to find out. Being diagnosed gave me new context on many traits I had been told were flaws up to this point, just because I didn't fit a narrow definition of 'functional'. It's immeasurably improved my life!

4. Have your feelings about having autism changed over the years?

Not really. First I was relieved that I wasn't broken, now I'm just taking care of myself and doing my best to turn my experience into a constructive learning opportunity for other people.

5. Did you know that you were different in some way before you were told about being autistic?

I thought I was just fundamentally bad at everything before I got diagnosed. I thought I was a bad kind of different, instead of just different.

6. What advice would you give parents about telling their child about their autism diagnosis?

Lead with the fact that different doesn't mean bad – it just means different. We're all different, and autism is just another difference.

7. How do you feel about having more than one diagnosis?

I think if I had many more, coping with things might get a bit complicated; two is manageable enough. I could probably go and get assessed for a few more, but I'm doing well enough as it is.

8. In what ways has knowing about your autism diagnosis helped you (if any)?

It's made me a lot more confident and self-comfortable – I used to think I wasn't able to do anything, and now I know I can do, within reason, whatever I want! I just need to remember that there's no one right way to do anything, and there's always another way to get where I want.

Question 1: What actually is autism anyway? People talk about it like I'm supposed to understand. I have tried reading about it online but it's all very confusing

SHORT ANSWER

There is no short answer to this one.

LONGER ANSWER

You're right, it is all very confusing, even for professionals who are supposed to know what they are talking about. I myself am constantly learning new things about autism, being surprised by it, and reconfiguring my understanding of what I think I know about it.

> #Autism is the overwhelming, ecstatic pleasure of sharing and expounding on what you love most with other people. (Sara Luterman @slooterman, 7.15 pm, 1 April 2018)

> #Autism is dynamic quality in action, picking out notes in a song, losing oneself in an activity, deeply held passionate interests, battling services or just trying to understand a form, nature's answer to overconformity, a description of development, a culture, your best pals... (Damian Milton @milton_damian, 3.07 pm, 1 April 2018)

Autism is a complex, invisible condition which a person is born with. Autistic people are likely to communicate, understand and interact with the world in a different way to most. However, with current prevalence rates at around every 1 in 68 people, they are a very significant minority. Autistic people usually have difficulties and differences in communication and social skills. They probably also have certain behaviours that they do over and over again, and passionate interests. Sensory difficulties are common. Anxiety and related difficulties with change and the need for routine are also common. A significant percentage of autistic people also have an additional intellectual disability, which brings with it its own challenges. Autism is described as a spectrum because it affects different people in different ways at different times in different situations and to different degrees of severity.

There are actually *hundreds* of different genes linked to autism, which seem to interact with the environment in some way that we do not understand yet to cause autism.

Current research indicates that what we now call autism is in fact lots of different conditions that look similar but have different origins.

'I'm autistic, which means everyone around me has a disorder that makes them say things they don't mean, not care about structure, fail to hyperfocus on singular important topics, have unreliable memories, drop weird hints and creepily stare into my eyeballs.'

'So why do people say YOU'RE the weird one?'

'Because there's more of them than me.'

(@autisticnotweird Autistic Not Weird Facebook post)

Some autistic advocates have asked, since there are so many of them, why should *they* be considered 'disordered'? Most autistic advocates right now say that autism is both a disability and also a different and equally valid way to be in this world. They also note that many of the more significant difficulties faced by autistic people actually come from factors *associated with* autism rather than autism itself (for example an added intellectual disability or epilepsy), as well as coming from the difficulties they face living in a society organised for neurotypical people.

Most autism advocates feel that it is important that we still think of autism as a 'condition' or 'disability' because of how difficult autism can be to live with, and so that autistic people can get extra help.

Some differences are on the outside of the person, like different colour hair or skin.
    Some differences are on the inside, sometimes in the brain.
    Autism is one of these differences.

Question 2: What do I call it? Is it autism, autism spectrum disorder or Asperger's syndrome? What about PDD-NOS? Different professionals and parents on online forums seem to use different words for it

SHORT ANSWER

Call it autism. He is autistic. She is on the autism spectrum.

LONGER ANSWER

There is a lot of confusion around autism terminology, for very good reason. Let me break it all down for you a bit:

Asperger's syndrome was a diagnosis that started being used in 1994. Until relatively recently, a child would have been diagnosed with Asperger's if they were showing signs of autism (for example, flapping, liking to play alone and finding it difficult to have a back and forth conversation) but their early language was not delayed and they had at least an average IQ (intelligence quotient). Another child showing the same flapping, liking to play alone and with conversation difficulties, but slow to talk and scoring below average on an IQ test, was instead given a diagnosis of **autism**.

Pervasive developmental disorder (PDD-NOS) was a diagnosis that *used* to be given when a child was showing some, but not all, signs of autism (so maybe they were flapping, liked to play alone but had great conversation skills).

However, in reality, all of this was very subjective, and the diagnosis you were given (Asperger's, autism or PDD-NOS) could change depending on the professional you went to. Throw into the mix the diversity seen in autism with IQ and language levels, and the many co-occurring conditions like attention deficit hyperactivity disorder, and the whole 'what type of autism do they fit in' decision was becoming unreliable, confusing and unhelpful for everyone involved, including autism researchers.

This led the American Psychiatric Association (APA) recently to *remove* the category of Asperger's syndrome altogether, and establish **autism spectrum disorder** as a new umbrella term. This meant that professionals (including myself) no longer needed to fit the great diversity that we see in clinical practice into a rigid subgroup. Autism spectrum disorder is often shortened to just **autism**. Some people shorten it to **ASD**. You will also hear people use '**on the spectrum**', which usually refers to the autism spectrum.

Lots of people previously diagnosed with Asperger's syndrome were very unhappy with the APA for erasing their diagnosis. Many spoke out about how having Asperger's (sometimes called being an '**Aspie**') was an important part of their identity, and was helpful in separating them from autistic people who were more significantly affected (for example those with no verbal language and an additional intellectual disability).

However, even more recently information has come to light that Hans Asperger (the Austrian paediatrician whose work with autistic children led to Asperger's syndrome being named after him) may have colluded with the Nazi eugenics programme during World War II. This has been disturbing for the autistic community, who as a group care deeply about acceptance, neurodiversity and inclusivity for all. The ongoing use of this term is therefore currently being hotly debated.

If your child has already been given a diagnosis of Asperger's syndrome I certainly don't think this whole 'autism vs Asperger's' debate is something you need to burden them with (although it is helpful for *you* to be aware of what is going on in the background). I think it's probably best just to let them decide which they prefer for now. They can make up their own minds from an informed place when they are older.

Although not recognised in the manuals that professionals use to diagnose autism, pathological demand avoidance (PDA) is a proposed subtype of autism, or what some call 'a behavioural profile within the autism spectrum'. The proposed PDA criteria has many similarities and some differences to what could be called a 'classic' autism profile (although of course autism itself is hugely diverse). Underpinning the difficulties experienced by children with this proposed profile is an intense anxiety, which leads to the child avoiding even simple demands. Some implications for support include that traditionally successful approaches with autistic people (for example visual schedules) are not effective with children with anxiety-based demand avoidance, as they perceive them to be demands in themselves.

There has also been a lot of debate about whether autism spectrum disorder (ASD) should instead be called **autism spectrum condition (ASC)** because of the stigmatising nature of the word 'disorder'. It is also currently being hotly debated whether autism is a difference, a disability or indeed both (which currently appears to be the point of view of most autistic advocates and scholars). For you as a parent, when talking to your child about autism first, I would recommend just using the terms 'autism' or 'autism spectrum'.

Question 3: What about all this 'autistic person' versus 'person with autism' stuff? What is the right way to say it?

SHORT ANSWER

At the moment, I use 'autistic person' because it is what most autistic people seem to prefer.

LONGER ANSWER

You have probably already noticed that I have been using terms like 'autistic child' in this book. This is called 'identity first' language. It is not currently the norm for how we talk about autism and other disabilities, and so I am aware that it can sound harsh to parents' ears. Like all language, the words we use when talking about disability are constantly evolving, and words that were commonplace (for example 'retarded') are now unacceptable. Up until very recently professionals (including myself) wishing to be respectful used mostly 'person first' language, that is, 'a child *with* autism'.

There is a good bit of debate going on about this very thing in the autism community right now, but the majority of autistic advocates do seem to prefer identity first language, that is, 'an autistic child'. They say that this is because autism is not something they carry along 'with' them (like a bag) and is not something that they could or should get rid of (like cancer). It is an integral part of them. Any autistic adult I have asked about this says they prefer 'autistic person'.

However, this *is* a large and diverse community, and I am sure that there are plenty of autistic people who prefer person first language. If you are unsure about what to use when talking to an autistic person, you can just respectfully ask them.

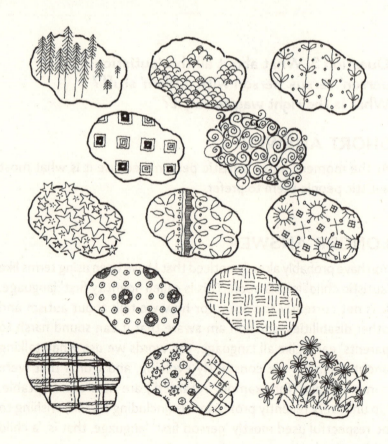

Question 4: Is he high or low functioning? Where on the autism scale does she fall?

SHORT ANSWER

There is no autism 'scale' and the terms high and low functioning (although often used by professionals) often end up being meaningless and stigmatising. Autism is a spectrum; everyone on it is different.

LONGER ANSWER

While it is understandably comforting for parents to hear that their child is only mildly affected by autism, in actuality, the use of scales and categories like high and low functioning are often unhelpful and misleading.

A *scale* implies that on one end we have people who are uniformly and at all times only very mildly affected by autism, and on the other end we have people who have all the difficulties, all of the time. But this is not how autism works. Instead, autism affects different people in different ways, at different times, in different situations and to different degrees of severity. That is why it is called a *spectrum*.

Autism isn't a linear spectrum of high or low. It's a whole bunch of different traits that are on their own spectrums. Kind of a 3D, weird mess. (Kirsten, diagnosed at 19 years old, *What Women with Autism Want You to Know*: Iris, YouTube)

The descriptions high and low functioning tell us nothing about a child's personality, their learning style, their individual difficulties, their individual traits or abilities or anything else that matters.

You might think that a young autistic man who has been studying astrophysics for fun since the age of seven is high functioning, but what if he experiences such severe anxiety that he can't leave his house? Is he 'higher functioning' than a different young autistic man who attended a special school, helps out in a pet shop part time and has friends he meets up with every week for a movie and a pizza?

Autistic advocates often say that to be labelled 'low functioning' results in low expectations and segregation, and to be labelled 'high functioning' results in people not believing how significantly affected they are by autism, and so expecting them to struggle through difficult situations, often to the detriment of their mental health. They speak about the 'ableism' inherent in these terms, how they imply that to be autistic and to openly show autistic traits (e.g. flapping) is wrong in itself and means someone is 'lower' than another. As one autistic woman said (in a YouTube video called *Shutting Down Bullsh*t on Autism 2*, which I urge you to watch): 'High functioning doesn't have to do with how disabled someone is. It is to do with how well they pass as neurotypical.'

Autistic people (like *all* people) fluctuate as to when they need help, and what kind of help they need. This is why the umbrella term of autism spectrum is so helpful. It allows people to be individuals, who will need support at different times of their lives, individual to them.

Some terminology

When I talk about the **autism community** in this book I am referring to autistic authors, advocates and activists from all over the world who speak out about autism and autistic rights. For example, the Autistic Self Advocacy Network is a prominent advocacy group within the autism community. However, I am also referring to all of the 'ordinary' autistic people I speak to every day, and follow on Twitter and other social media platforms. This is, of course, a huge and diverse group of people.

Neurotypical is a word to describe a person with a so-called 'typical' brain: people without autism, mental illness or neurological differences.

Ableism is a word to describe the discrimination or prejudice against people with disabilities, including autism.

An example of their use:

The belief that behaving in a **neurotypical** way is inherently better than behaving in an autistic way is described as **ableist** by the **autism community**.

Question 5: But aren't we all a little bit autistic?

SHORT ANSWER
No.

LONGER ANSWER

The great thing about the 'Aren't we all a bit autistic?' sentiment is that it always comes from a place of love and acceptance and an embracing of difference. Parents may have heard about autistic people liking order, or needing to be alone sometimes, and recognised those things in themselves. Sometimes the parents who say it are autistic themselves, or have similar traits, and so many of their child's behaviours seem typical within their own family context and personal history.

Neurotypical people can of course experience similar difficulties to autistic people. We are all human and have more in common than different. There are also lots of children who show autistic traits (for example, finger tapping, sensory issues and an intense preoccupation with Harry Potter) but ultimately they have a few friends, they get on OK in school and work and in general are happy. As Temple Grandin has said, 'When does nerd turn into Asperger?' (*The World Needs All Kinds of Brains*, TedTalk by Temple Grandin on YouTube). But these children are unlikely to be given a diagnosis of autism because under the current diagnostic criteria (and it is very important to be aware that diagnostic criteria change all of the time) autistic traits need to be *very* significantly impacting on the person's life. This means that people currently diagnosed as autistic have 'disabling' experiences that go beyond what the majority of people experience. If they did not, they would not have been diagnosed in the first place. Many autistic advocates have spoken out about how unhelpful and possibly irrelevant this diagnostic criteria and process is, which leads to many people who self identify as autistic being told by professionals that their symptoms are not severe enough to 'qualify'.

Many autistic people have spoken out about the phrase 'We are all a bit autistic' saying that it trivialises and negates the very real challenges that they face on a daily basis. Because if we are all on the spectrum, and we all experience similar levels of discomfort, then why do they find certain things so difficult? Why are shopping centres terrifying? Why are they the target of bullying? Why can't they cope with homework? Why should they get extra support in college?

I knew that I was too different to be normal, and every time I tried to say that, people just wouldn't listen, and it was just 'Oh, everyone is unique' and all that, which is rubbish actually. Because there are people who are more unique and need help. (Kesia in *Autism Documentary: Inside the UK's Only School for Autistic Girls*, Channel 4 News – a recommended watch)

CHAPTER 2

Do I Really Need to Tell Them They Are Autistic?

Q&A AMELIE, AGED 8

1. What age were you when you found out about your autism diagnosis?

I was eight years old.

2. How did you find out?

My parents told me. They were talking to me for a long time about people who were different and stuff. One day I asked was I 'different' and they said yes you have Asperger's and explained what it was. The strengths and the challenges.

3. How did you feel about it when you did find out?

I felt disappointed at the time.

4. Have your feelings about having autism changed since you first heard about it?

Yes. I feel now that is part of who I am and that it is not my fault.

5. Did you know that you were different in some way before you were told about being autistic?

Yes. I always felt a bit different and I felt it hard to fit in.

6. What advice would you give parents about telling their child about their autism diagnosis?

Not make it sound like a big deal. To let them know there are good sides to it as well. If the child sees it negatively and talks to you about it, always remember to remind them if that is what they want to think that is the way it might happen but if they think positively things will turn out more positive.

7. Have you read any books about autism that you think explain autism well?

Different Like Me – My Autism Heroes (Jessica Kingsley Publishers) worked for me. It showed a lot of famous people who had traits I could relate to.

8. In what ways has knowing about your autism diagnosis helped you (if any)?

I know the things I can improve on. But not just that – now I know the good things about me and how to make them better.

Question 6: Do I really need to tell him he is autistic?

SHORT ANSWER

Yes, I think you do. Without a diagnosis your child is still autistic, just without the tools to understand or cope with it. He needs to understand himself. He needs to link in with other autistic people. Autistic people unanimously agree it's better to know. Not telling him may have a negative impact on his future mental health.

LONGER ANSWER

And please do not think this is a bad thing, this is THE BEST DIAGNOSIS I'VE EVER HAD. It's been like being given the lid to the jigsaw puzzle of 10,000 pieces that I've been working on for decades. So I can see the whole picture for the first time. #ActuallyAutistic (wildrenaissance @WildRenaissance, 1.33 am, 15 December 2018)

─────────────

I spend the majority of my working week with autistic children and teenagers. I find them to be kind, creative and funny. They are often hugely empathic and sensitive and so feel their own emotions deeply (oftentimes *too* deeply). I love the way they cut through social niceties and artifice. I love the outside of the box way they come at ideas. They often worry a lot about the world, and care deeply about social justice and fairness, which is an admirable but difficult path for a child to follow. They want friendships and romance and a job just the same as everyone else. They generally hate school. They are some of my favourite people in the world.

Sometimes I meet these children for their diagnostic assessment and have the pleasure of helping them on their journey of understanding and accepting autism. But sometimes I meet them many years after their diagnosis when they come for some emotional support. These children's experiences of how autism was explained to them (if at all) vary greatly.

Although all of these children still experience the challenges associated with autism, the children whose parents told them at a young age and in whose homes autism is discussed openly and matter of factly as a normal part of everyday life stand out. These children can still speak negatively about autism (quite frequently in fact!) but they have adjusted to their diagnosis with more ease, are better able to engage in the therapeutic process because of a greater self-awareness, are better able to advocate for themselves in school and in their communities, and so often manage themselves better in difficult situations.

They typically have a more realistic image of themselves (both their strengths and their challenges) and their sense of themselves and their identity is on a more stable ground. They are often more positive about a future after school when they can focus on their special interests (for example in a job or in college). All of these are important protective factors for mental health difficulties in later life.

While I can see clearly the different reasons parents choose *not* to tell their children (and I have hopefully addressed many of these in this book), I cannot recall a single autistic person I have spoken to who has conveyed an understanding as to why a parent would choose not to tell their child they are autistic. They say things like 'That's like not telling someone they are a boy or a girl' or 'Why would they not tell them, it's like they think we have a disease or something, it's just autism!' and 'It's a child's right to know. Not telling should not be an option. It's not like there is something wrong with you, you're just different. My parents not talking about it made me think that it was something to hide or be ashamed of.'

This last comment is hugely important in the context of this book. If you choose not to tell your child about their diagnosis, or you tell them once and never mention it again, what message are you giving them about autism? By your omission are you actually telling them that autism is something to be ashamed of? Something that makes you so uncomfortable that you can't even say the word out loud?

The last thing that you want is your child being told about their diagnosis by someone else unwittingly, or for them to learn about it by seeing a letter or report with their diagnosis on it (which I have known to happen, with very negative consequences for family relationships). Another very serious issue to consider is that by not talking about autism you are also leaving your child open to learning about autism in general from other sources, which may not come at the subject as lovingly or positively as you would. You are also leaving them open to picking up all kinds of false information and beliefs about autism that by not talking about it will continue to go unchallenged.

My mum sat me down for a serious talk. I freaked out because it was like she was telling me I had cancer or something. I don't know why she did that because it wasn't bad news she was giving me. It was the opposite! (Chloe, 25)

A great many autistic adults have documented unhappy and confusing childhoods followed by the relief and joy that came with a late diagnosis and the benefits that this provided, including more and truer friendships and increased self-acceptance. They say that learning about their diagnosis gave them a sense of belonging and an identity. They talk about finding their tribe, a community of people who understand and like them just as they are. They say that it helped other people understand them better, which led to improvements in how people treated them. They use analogies like a cement coat being unbuttoned, or finding out they were not an alien. They talk about realising they are not 'pathetic or weak'.

Here are some very typical comments from autistic adults that I have heard or read:

- 'I wish I had been diagnosed as a child. If I had known why all that stuff was going on in my head it would have helped me to feel like less of a weirdo.'

- 'For years I saw myself as broken and spent my whole life trying to fix myself. Getting a diagnosis was the best thing I ever did. Now I can get the right kind of support.'

- 'I spent my whole life not knowing the reason why I was weird, odd, rejected, outcast and not coping. I wish I had known earlier why I was different, then perhaps I would have been able to cope better and had access to help. It would have helped me to know that the reason for my difference was a wiring difference and not because there is something wrong with me, or it was my fault.'

- 'As soon as I read the description I knew it was me. It was a huge relief. My life made sense. It explained so much. I didn't know other people don't struggle with the things that I do.'

I know many autistic people who choose not to tell other people that they have autism and they have many different valid reasons for this. But even these people believe that it was important and vital that they themselves were told.

Question 7: I know he is autistic, but I don't want to tell him or other people. I don't want him to be labelled

SHORT ANSWER

The problem is not the label of autism, which is just a neutral description. The problem is with society's current attitude towards autism. Helping your child to understand autism in an empowering way will give him the *right* information to help him to fight back against any potential stigma.

LONGER ANSWER

Not wanting their child to be 'labelled' is a real and genuine concern for parents, who ask me about this a lot. However, many autistic advocates have expressed an intense frustration with the word 'label' being used about their own autism diagnosis. They instead say things like:

> To be honest I don't care if it's a diagnosis or a label. I am just relieved that I am simply autistic and not a bad, lazy, broken failure. (Mary, 25)

and

> Autism was the 'label' that set me free to be myself, although I prefer 'identified' to 'labelled'. I was never neuro-typical, label or no label. Being identified as #autistic was simply & naturally that – finding my own identity, after half a century of copying other people. (Cos @autismage, 5.25 pm, 8 January 2018)

However, what autistic people do quite rightly take issue with is being defined by a negative, outdated and unhelpful view of autism and disability.

So, let's unpack this one a bit.

First, and prepare yourself because I'm going to be really blunt here, with or without an official diagnosis, autistic children are already being labelled. They are calling themselves weird and stupid. Other children sense their difference and are unsettled by it because they don't understand it – they'll have their own names and labels. Teachers are calling them lazy, rude, hyperactive, difficult, challenging and uncooperative. Professionals with little understanding of autism are suggesting all kinds of incorrect diagnoses, with a knock-on effect of them not accessing the right supports.

In my experience, getting an autism diagnosis actually *decreases* negative labelling. When people know that a child has autism, their behaviour is no longer seen as weird, or difficult, but is instead understood, and they start being kinder and more patient.

Next, let's look at the term 'giving a label', which implies that some kind of burdensome *thing* has been *given* to your child by the person who made the diagnosis. But the truth is that children are not 'given' autism, in the same way that they are not 'given' being gay, deaf, brown haired or Irish. Your child was always autistic; it has just been confirmed.

If your child is autistic, they are always going to be autistic. They are not choosing to be how they are and they can't choose to stop being autistic. It is as much an integral part of them as their gender.

However, your child is also more than their autism. They are their own person, with their own family, history, experiences, thoughts, emotions, personality, temperament, resilience, stubbornness and will. Being given a diagnosis of autism does not mean your child will suddenly lose all of these. They will be the same child before and after the diagnosis.

When the autism diagnosis *does* become a problem is when a child, or the people around them, start seeing and treating them as if autism defines the totality of who they are. It is a problem if everything that a child says or does is put down to 'their autism'. This is something that people with a range of disabilities know all too well.

To avoid your child's diagnosis being used as a label, continue to treat them as the individual that they are, and encourage other people to do so too. Tell them about the 'label' autism, but do this in the context of all the other labels that together define them, including all the positive labels. Let them follow their passions, and help them have areas in their life in which they can succeed and flourish. This will go a long way towards them developing an identity that is not all about their disability or difference.

Question 8: My child has a few different diagnoses. Which ones do I tell her about? It seems too much to tell her about all of them

SHORT ANSWER

Personally, I think start with the one that affects her the most. Definitely at some point tell her about the autism, and add on the others over time only if needed or helpful.

LONGER ANSWER

When children have a long list of diagnoses, it brings into focus how little we understand about difference and disability, and the whole point of diagnosis in the first place. In an ideal world, *all* children would receive the support they need without the need for any diagnosis. But back in the real world most children need them to access public resources (for example, occupational therapy in the case of dyspraxia or mental health services in the case of depression).

Many children on the autism spectrum have several different diagnoses. Sometimes these additional diagnoses are helpful. For example, if we know a child also has dyslexia it means we can look up the most recent dyslexia research to see what helps. A child attending a mainstream school will see clearly the extra work they need to put into literacy and know this has nothing to do with autism. Not telling them about dyslexia would just be confusing for them.

However, often the additional diagnoses are *not* helpful, and clearly it is not going to be good for your child to be given a long list of names explaining what is 'wrong' with them, reinforcing the view that the problem lies only with them and has nothing to do with our wider society.

Which diagnoses you choose to tell them, and in what order, is going to be very dependent on individual circumstances. I have had clients with very significant attention and hyperactivity difficulties who benefited more from having their ADHD diagnosis explained to them first. I have had other clients for whom, although they also had a previous diagnosis of ADHD, their social and communication difficulties were their greatest needs, and it was felt that it would be better for their parents to concentrate on the autism diagnosis to start with. It is worth noting that in my professional experience I have seen many children diagnosed early with both autism and ADHD, who later in life (while clearly still autistic) would most likely no longer meet the criteria for ADHD.

Tip

If your child is aware of their many different diagnoses, make sure to emphasise to them just how NORMAL this is for lots of autistic people (as indeed it is).

My advice would be to start with the one that is causing the most difficulty at the moment, and for which they are receiving help. Over time work towards telling them about autism. And then decide on a case by case basis whether there is any need for them to know about the additional diagnoses.

However, an important exception to this is if your child is experiencing significant mental health issues, for example an additional anxiety or mood disorder. In these cases, an understanding of autism will be vital to your child understanding themselves and their difficulties and I strongly recommend that both be explained to them.

A final observation on additional diagnoses: it is positive at least that mental health issues are now starting to be recognised as separate to autism – as in the past once a child was given an autism diagnosis it was assumed that all mood or behavioural issues were 'just a part of the autism', meaning that they missed out on vital understanding and support.

CHAPTER 3

Won't Telling Them Just Make Them Feel Different?

Q&A JANE, AGED 31

1. What age were you when you found out about your autism diagnosis?

> When my son was diagnosed at six I kept telling the team that yes, he does x, y or z but that's normal, sure I used to do it. The psychologist just pursed her lips and said, 'It's an indication of autism.' It wasn't until four years later when I was 30 and I understood more about autism that I decided to seek a formal diagnosis.

2. How did you find out?

> I slowly started to realise that I had many of the same characteristics as my son who was diagnosed at six, and over time the more I learnt about how females present the more I felt it matched me. I sought a formal diagnosis at 30.

3. How did you feel about it when you did find out?

It explained a lot for me. I sought out the adult autism community and they have been great at helping me understand myself. I also occasionally go to a women's autism meet up which is nice.

4. Have your feelings about having autism changed over the years?

When my son was diagnosed I didn't believe them and sought a second opinion. Once I accepted his diagnosis and understood what autism is, I saw it in myself. Since my diagnosis I have met so many amazing people in the adult autism community, that it's a community that I am proud to be part of. However, although I have told my occupational health department (who were extremely supportive and noted that some of the aspects of my autism enhance my professional abilities) and I've told some close friends, I've had mixed reaction. I fell out with one friend so I am reluctant to name it with other people as many people have a misconception as to what autism is. My friends and colleagues who don't know my diagnosis would however describe me as unique, so I think deep inside they know I am autistic even if they can't put a word to it.

5. Did you know that you were different in some way before you were told about being autistic?

I always felt different even as a child. I would be described as quiet and I always felt like an outsider. I learnt to mask and fit in and I studied people and their behaviour (which I'm pretty good at reading now). I can fit in with people now and make eye contact (which is physically painful) but I know it's a social expectation and I am able to meet the expectations that society has for me, and I'm more willing to do it now that I know why I experience things differently.

6. What advice would you give parents about telling their child about their autism diagnosis?

Discover what autism means together. What made me proud of my diagnosis was meeting other people like me and understanding that autism doesn't stop me from succeeding, it just allows me to take a different path to success.

7. Have you read any books about autism that you think explain autism well?

I like books by autistic people like Michael Barton and Stephen Shore.

8. How do you feel about having more than one diagnosis?

I have autism and dyslexia. I discovered I have dyslexia when I was 18 in college; I find that having dyslexia is more socially acceptable than having autism.

9. In what ways has knowing about your autism diagnosis helped you (if any)?

It's helped me to understand why I see the world differently and to embrace my autistic strengths. It has also allowed me to meet a community of wonderful people just like me who have similar challenges and can give great advice to me.

Question 9: She works so hard at fitting in – won't a diagnosis make her feel different?

SHORT ANSWER

Yes, it will. But she is already different. Through knowing about her diagnosis, she can meet other autistic children who are different in the same way as she is. It will help her understand and embrace these differences. Her increased self-awareness and acceptance will most likely lead to better, truer friendships with both neurotypical and autistic people.

LONGER ANSWER

I survived 57 years of masking & camouflaging but the toll was affecting my health to the point where I sought answers & ultimately a diagnosis of #Autism. (Autism Tweets @AutismTweetsUK, 10.01 am, 30 October 2018)

The phrase you don't look 'Autistic' is not helpful. It can be offensive. It deserves one response. 'You don't look like a nob but here we are.' (Claire Hooton @RockingAutism73, 3.08 am, 3 January 2019)

I have met a few very wise and lucky autistic children who have no interest in fitting in, who fly their own flag and don't particularly care what other people think of them. As one boy so succinctly put it, 'What's so great about being a sheep?' However, unfortunately these children are rare, and the vast majority of autistic children I know care very deeply about being accepted by their peers and the hurt is deep and damaging for those who are not.

Caring about how other people see us, and the importance of fitting in and being accepted by our peers, is very normal for older children and rises sharply during adolescence (it is interesting to note this has also been seen in the behaviour of other mammals including mice). However, to all of our relief, this tends to decrease again in early adulthood.

If your child is putting a lot of effort into fitting in, some good questions to ask yourself are: How is this working out for her? Are the friendships that she is working so hard to sustain *genuine* and bringing her happiness? How much of herself is she having to hide or mask in order to sustain these friendships? How much energy is all of this taking out of her?

Masking is a term commonly used when autistic people hide their autistic traits (for example, not allowing themselves to jump in public or making eye contact during conversation even if it hurts them). Masking takes a significant amount of energy and comes at a cost. It is something that most autistic people do to some degree, but appears to be much more commonly used by autistic women. Unfortunately, there is recent research to suggest that masking is linked to a significantly increased likelihood of mental health issues including depression, anxiety and even suicide.

Autistic children need to be given the message from everyone around them that they do not need to hide behind a mask or act neurotypically in order to be loved and accepted. They need to be given the message that there is nothing wrong with being autistic, and that 'acting autistic' is a valued way to be.

Learning about her autism will help your child understand and love her differences. It will provide her with a community of people who understand her and with whom she won't have to work so hard at fitting in. Realising that she does not need to live her life like a neurotypical person and to neurotypical standards will help her be happier and more relaxed, with the ironic consequences of being able to function better in a neurotypical environment and enjoy neurotypical friends.

Think critically about therapies

Autism therapies in the past have focused on reducing stereotypy and other 'autistic behaviours', that is, their aim was for the child to look and behave more like their neurotypical peers.

However, in the context of learning to accept and embrace their autistic differences, there is no point telling your child that being autistic is a valued way to be, if you are then bringing them to therapy where the main focus is on them hiding their autism and behaving neurotypically.

Therapy should help parents and children build on strengths and make life easier and happier for everyone. It should help autistic people to understand and embrace their neurological differences. It should take into account the voices of autistic people, and specific therapy 'programmes' should ideally be created in collaboration with the autistic community. Therapy should also aim to build autism-friendly families and communities (so the onus is not all on the child to change **their** behaviour). Also, very importantly, children should **enjoy** therapy sessions, not only because it is respectful and best practice, but also because children learn best when they are happy.

It is very interesting (and recommended) to research online about what the autism community think about even well-established therapies associated with autism.

Question 10: Won't she start using autism as an excuse to get out of things that she doesn't like?

SHORT ANSWER

Yes, she might. However, it is more helpful to see autism as a possible *reason* for some of the things she finds difficult, rather than an excuse. Teach her to advocate for herself instead.

LONGER ANSWER

Children resist doing things that they find difficult.

If there is something your child really does not want to do and she is letting you know all about it, instead of thinking that she is being stubborn or challenging, take a deep breath and think of it as her way of telling you that she is really struggling and needs help. Reframing how you think about her behaviours in this way will not only be more likely to bring about change, it will also help reduce your own frustration and anger (and let's face it, all parents need a bit of help with that sometimes). Because being autistic *does not* mean that your child *can't* do things that other children can, but it *does* mean that she will *need extra help* along the way. And knowing about and understanding autism is a big part of helping her get there.

Let's look in more detail at an example of something you might be afraid your child will use an excuse:

I can't go to Granny's party because of my autism.

In this case it is very likely that your child's difficulty with Granny's party is genuine. Many (not all!) autistic children find the loud, crowded, unpredictable, social nature of parties just too much to deal with.

In this scenario, autism might genuinely be one of the *reasons* she doesn't want to go to Granny's party (for example, because of sensory or social challenges) but it doesn't have to be an excuse to not celebrate her grandmother's birthday or go to a party ever again. There are other ways to show someone you love them on their birthday: making them a card or meeting up the next day for a cupcake. And there are plenty of ways to make parties a bit more bearable, for example only going for ten minutes, or wearing ear defenders.

I recommend looking at these excuses instead as great *opportunities* to teach your child to *advocate* for herself (which means using skills to get what you need out of life). So instead of saying 'I don't want to go to Granny's party because of my autism', teach her to say:

- 'I'm a bit worried about the noise at Granny's party. Can I bring headphones?'

- 'I really don't like it when there are lots of people there. Can I play in the hall with Lego?'

- 'Granny's. Ten minutes. Then home.'

Learning how to advocate for herself will continue throughout her life, and needs to be taught in school as well as at home. It will mean being able to ask her teacher to turn off a flickering light so that she can listen in class, telling a doctor that she doesn't like light touch so that she can be properly examined when sick, or telling a lecturer that she has dyspraxia and absolutely cannot produce that hand-written essay they asked for, but absolutely *can* provide a great typed one.

A great starting point for developing advocacy skills is involving children in their individual education plans (IEPs) and allowing them to have input into what they feel would be helpful for them in the school environment.

So instead of seeing an autism diagnosis as something your child might use as an excuse not to progress, instead start looking at it as something that, with your help and guidance, will provide her with a deeper understanding of herself and her needs, and will also provide her with the tools to be happier and more successful in her life.

Some autistic people choose to self-disclose about autism (i.e. tell people outright that they are autistic) when they are advocating for themselves, for example, 'I have autism, so I need to wear sunglasses in here because of the fluorescent lights.' Many others choose not to name the autism but still advocate for themselves, for example, 'Sorry, it might seem a bit strange but I need to wear sunglasses in here because the fluorescent lights hurt my eyes.' I would recommend giving your child the choice, but being careful to present both of the options as equally valid (so they don't get the impression that there is something wrong with telling people they are autistic).

CHAPTER 4

How Do I Actually Go about Telling My Child that They Are Autistic?

Q&A SAM, AGED 8

1. What age were you when you found out about your autism diagnosis?

Seven.

2. How did you find out?

Assessments.

3. How did you feel about it when you did find out?

A bit nervous.

4. Have your feelings about having autism changed since then?

Yes. I'm more encouraged and I'm happier now because I've got an SNA (special needs assistant).

5. Did you know that you were different in some way before you were told about being autistic?

Yes.

6. What advice would you give parents about telling their child about their autism diagnosis?

Tell them they're autistic because they might not understand why they're different.

7. How do you feel about having more than one diagnosis? (Sam also has dyspraxia and dyslexia.)

Not that bad.

8. Have you read any books or seen any videos that you think explain autism well?

There was one (a video) in class but it wasn't very good.

9. In what ways has knowing about your autism diagnosis helped you (if any)?

I understand myself better.

Question 11: When is the best time to tell him?

SHORT ANSWER

The earlier the better, but it's never too late.

LONGER ANSWER

I have already discussed all the ways that autistic adults have felt their lives have improved since learning about their diagnosis, and the confusion not knowing caused them. Their accounts clearly show the importance of telling your child as soon as possible. I have also already discussed how difficult the teenage years can be, when conformity and other people's opinions become magnified in their importance. In my experience, if you have the option of telling your child before all of this kicks in, I strongly recommend you take it.

Certainly, if your child is showing awareness of their difference and expressing frustration or confusion about why they think or act different to other people, they need to hear about it as soon as possible. 'Why can't I be like everyone else?', 'Why am I in a special class/school?', 'What is wrong with everyone?', 'I'm so stupid', 'I'm the only person in the class without friends', 'Nobody likes the same things as me' are all indicators that your child is finding it difficult to understand their experiences without knowing about his diagnosis.

However, this of course does not mean sitting down your toddler for a big serious TALK, and what you tell a five-year-old is going to be very different to what you tell a teenager. So, let's go straight to talking about how you can go about it.

Question 12: OK, I'm ready. Now how do I actually go about it? I don't have a clue what to do or say!

SHORT ANSWER

1. Start talking about neurodiversity.

2. Start talking about strengths.

3. Be the air steward you want to see.

4. Rethink autistic 'problems'.

5. Make sure they see, hear and learn about other autistic people.

6. Use books and videos.

7. Write out your own personalised explanation.

8. Try some creative, visual activities.

LONGER ANSWER
Start talking about neurodiversity

Neurodiversity (seen by some as a socio-political movement and by some as a more neutral way to describe neurological difference) is a concept in which *all* neurological differences (including for example dyspraxia, dyslexia, autism and attention deficit hyperactivity disorder (ADHD)) are recognised and respected as part of the natural variability of being human. Neurodiversity is based on the belief that there is *no such thing as normal* when it comes to human beings, and that diversity is an essential ingredient in a thriving natural environment and is valuable in its own right.

A nice way of describing different brains with a neurodiversity focus is to use analogies like different operating systems, for example, 'Autism is not a processing *error*, it's just a different processing *system*. Like Android versus Apple.'

Perhaps the most valuable message arising from the concept of neurodiversity is that autistic children do not have to spend their lives 'fixing' themselves in order to fit in with some neurotypical ideal.

There is some concern and debate within the autism community that if the focus becomes *too* much about neurodiversity, and autism stops being looked at as a disorder (i.e. it is seen as just another human variation like eye colour), autistic people will lose access to necessary specialist support (as this money is often ringfenced for people with disabilities). However, as a concept that will help normalise autism and neurological differences in your family, neurodiversity is very helpful, and I personally try to embrace a neurodiversity perspective whilst also continuing to emphasise that autistic people still need added support.

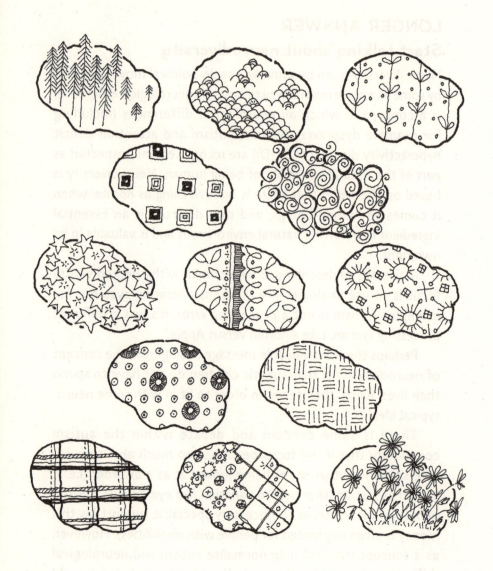

At home, start talking about neurodiversity and difference in general terms in normal conversation. Normalise different terms for difference and disability in your home. In general conversations, begin linking this back to your own wider family, saying things like 'Auntie Bea is amazing at tennis. She has dyslexia, so it was hard for her to learn to read.' 'Your dad is so active, he finds it hard to sit still even to watch a movie. He gets things done really quickly.' Eventually, work your way around to saying something like, 'You know the way you love video games but you hate birthday parties? There's a name for that – it's autism.'

For some further reading on this topic, and the history of autism, read the excellent **NeuroTribes: The Legacy of Autism and the Future of Neurodiversity** by Steve Silberman (Avery).

You know the way there are lots of different animals and plants? Well, there are lots of different kinds of human brains too. Autistic people's brains are wired a bit differently to most. Being different isn't a bad thing. In fact, being and thinking differently can be a really good thing. Lots of great inventors and artists are autistic. It allows them to come up with new ideas that have never been thought of before.

Start talking about strengths

Although the concept of neurodiversity embraces the multitude of differences that exist within the human mind, in order to be given a diagnosis of autism, you have unfortunately most likely been through a difficult diagnostic process that focused on all the things your child struggles with, all the ways that make them different from other people and the negative effects of autism on their lives and wellbeing. Your child's diagnostic report is probably full of these negatives and differences too (although good ones will focus also on positives and strengths). Unfortunately, this is the reality of accessing an autism diagnosis today, as it is necessary for diagnosticians to show clearly what areas of a child's life are being significantly impacted by autistic traits.

However, when looking into history it is clear that there are autistic traits which are highly beneficial and have advanced our society and thinking. Autistic people have been our astronauts, scientists, doctors, engineers, musicians, inventors, writers, artists and mathematicians. While many autistic people have learning difficulties, many are also exceptionally bright, and there is a proven link between autism and prodigy, for example sharing extraordinary memory skills.

In addition, it is a strengths-based focus (at home, in education and in therapies) that will lead to the best and happiest outcomes for your child. So now that the autism diagnosis has been confirmed, you're going to need to flip all of this negativity around and instead focus on and talk about the many positive traits that your child may have which are associated with neurodiversity and autism, like:

SUPERIOR HEARING AND SMELL

ATTENTION TO DETAIL

CARING ABOUT ANIMALS

KINDNESS

RETENTION OF FACTS

VISUAL SKILLS

HONESTY

PASSION

FOCUS

EXCELLENT MEMORY

LESS TIED TO SOCIETAL EXPECTATIONS

CARING ABOUT THE WORLD

CREATIVITY

STRONG MORALITY

AUTHENTICITY

STRONG SENSE OF JUSTICE AND FAIRNESS

IMAGINATION

PERFECTIONISM

LOYALTY

OUTSIDE THE BOX THINKING

For a great video on the reasons for focusing on strengths watch **The World Needs All Kinds of Brains,** Temple Grandin TedTalk on YouTube.

The book **Uniquely Human: A Different Way of Seeing Autism** by Barry M. Prizant (Simon & Schuster) is a wonderful, insightful and compassionate book which emphasises strengths.

I know you hate shopping centres. Lots of autistic people say it's like having super senses like Spiderman. You can see, hear and smell things lots of other people can't. So, when there is too much going on around you it can all get a bit too much. You are so amazing at knowing different smells — it's a very special skill to have.

You are so creative. I love all these new Pokémon characters you have created. Look how you drew all those tiny details. I see you spending a long time getting them just right. Lots of autistic people are really creative and good at focusing just like you. I know the kids in school don't like Pokémon any more but I met this great autistic guy the other day and he really loves Pokémon too! We might go and have a chat with him about Pokémon and autism next week. What do you think? He might have a few tips about working in animation for you.

Be the air steward you want to see

In contrast to the myth that autistic people lack empathy, in my experience they can be highly attuned to people's emotions and moods. In fact, autistic people can often be in many ways *over* sensitive, feeling everything that bit more intensely and experiencing shut down because of it.

With so much of communication being non-verbal, it is very important then not just to carefully choose the *words* you say about autism, but also that you are careful about your face, your tone of voice, your energy levels and your body language when doing so.

Let's imagine for a moment that you are in an airplane and it hits some turbulence. The plane starts bouncing, the fasten seatbelt lights come on. You (a nervous flyer) see the air steward coming down the aisle of the plane and decide to ask her what is going on. How would you like her to talk to you? Here are some options:

1. She sits beside you with a very serious face and tells you slowly that 'Everything is going to be absolutely FINE.'

2. She ignores your attempts to get her attention, and continues running down the plane shouting 'Everything is going to be absolutely fine!' as she checks and rechecks the exits frantically.

3. She pauses in her calm walk down the plane, puts her hand on your shoulder, and with a smile on her face tells you 'Everything is going to be absolutely fine. It's only a bit of minor turbulence, very normal. Now why don't I get you a cup of tea because you look like you need one, and then you can ask me any other questions you might have.'

When talking to your child about autism, be (or just pretend to be) that warm, in control and matter of fact air stewardess, guiding them on their journey, answering questions, *normalising* and calming as she goes.

Rethink autistic 'problems'

One of the most important pieces of advice I can give to parents is to start thinking critically about some of what are considered to be 'problems' with autism, and instead open yourself up to the possibility that the problem isn't with your child, but instead with societal systems and expectations. Thinking critically in this way will give you the language and the confidence to talk to your child about autism in positive ways that will help build their self-esteem and their understanding of themselves and the challenges they face.

Here are some examples:

PASSIONS

When *neurotypical* children show an exceptional skill in one area (for example violin, science or football) and spend a lot of time engaged in and talking about it, they are generally heaped with praise and encouraged as much as possible to pursue these interests through extra classes, competitions and camps. People encourage the child by asking them about it, and telling them how they are going to be famous or accomplished one day in this field. These children's interests are called 'passions' and 'gifts'.

However, often when an *autistic* child has a particular interest in something, knows a lot about it and wants to spend a lot of time doing it, it is called an 'obsession' and viewed in a negative way (which may not be surprising given that it is in fact one aspect of the diagnostic criteria for autism). Adults around the child can often speak negatively about the child's 'obsession' and work at reducing the child's engagement with it.

If *any* child is spending *all* their time doing one thing and they are missing out on other valuable learning opportunities, this is clearly something that needs support. However, we need to be careful of this double standard. Just because a child is autistic, it does not mean that their skill or interest is less extraordinary or special than if they were neurotypical. In fact, the most successful career choices for autistic people are in their area of passion, bringing not only employment but also joy, meaning and friendships through common interests. Autistic people talk about the intense pleasure that comes from spending time on their special interest, and how denying it to them has negative effects on their mental health.

Instead of thinking of your child's interests as an obsession that needs to be reduced, think of them as 'passions', let them enjoy them, and use them to motivate and engage them and interact with the world around them.

> I love the way you are so passionate about trains. There are lots of people out there who love trains as much as you do. Let's see if we can find them for you to talk to. Do you think you'd like to drive a train when you are older? You'd be so good at it!

SCHOOL

Everyone is a genius. But if you judge a fish by its ability to climb a tree, it will live its whole life believing it is stupid. (attributed to Albert Einstein)

In my experience, most autistic children (irrespective of their cognitive or language skills) find school exceptionally difficult. As a group, they experience very high rates of school refusal. The challenges they face are often looked at as autistic 'problems' that the child needs to overcome in order for them to fit into the system provided for them. And if a child can't cope with the noise, the micro humiliations, the extended periods of masking, sitting still and repressing repetitive movements, the sheer volume of academic information thrown at them and the daily isolation and exclusion, *they* are the ones made to feel like failures.

But in actuality, this is not *their* failure but the failure of a narrow and rigid western education system based on a production line mentality, with an emphasis on academics, conformity, obedience, body stillness, working towards the middle, retention of facts and assessment.

For an excellent talk on how our current education system is failing children, I would urge you to watch the short, narrated video from a talk by Ken Robinson called **RSA Animate: Changing Education Paradigms**, easily found on YouTube.

Instead of blaming children with autism and excluding them (both purposely and inadvertently) from our educational settings, we should be looking critically at and challenging a system that expects all children to achieve academic success in the very particular way that we expect them to and considers them to have failed if they don't. There are in fact a lot of very successful adults who did not follow a traditional school path, and certainly a qualification is no guarantee of employment in today's job market (although it does make things easier).

Let's instead start working towards neurodiversity-informed education, including rethinking our definitions of success, increasing flexibility within the system in general, allowing children to focus on their passions, providing mentors and vocational training, emphasising kindness and inclusion with *all* children, making meaningful links in the community and creating safe and comfortable sensory environments to work in.

Schools really care about sitting down in your seat, don't they? It's a bit ridiculous really. It's not normal to sit down all the time. I take lots of breaks to walk when I work. I even stand when working on my computer. You have loads of energy just like me. When you're older you can choose a job like mine where you can move around. But, for now, we need to get through school. Do you think it would help if we asked your teacher to send you on a job every ten minutes?

FOCUS

Autistic children often find it really difficult to move from one activity to another (often called transitioning). Autistic adults have told me that the issue is that they get so focused on the thing they are doing, it can actually be painful to move their focus suddenly to another thing. Instead of focusing on your child's difficulties transitioning, instead focus on the great concentration and focus they can have when they *are* engaged.

You are so good at concentrating. I see how strong your focus gets when you are playing your games. I know that turning off the TV is really difficult for you. But it would be great to be able to turn it off without you shouting at me. So I am going to use this timer to help you prepare. I will set it for three minutes and put it on top of the TV. You can watch it to see how much time you have left. When it goes off, then I will turn off the TV. If you are still feeling frustrated you could go jump on your trampoline for a while instead of shouting.

SENSE OF SOCIAL JUSTICE

For such a valuable and admirable personality trait, a strong sense of social justice can cause intense frustration for people who possess it, as many autistic people do. I have known children to talk angrily *years* after an incident in which their teacher gave a whole class punishment for the actions of one child.

However, instead of seeing and talking about your child's strong sense of justice as something negative, emphasise with them how valuable to the world this personality trait is. It will be a positive addition to their own sense of themselves, their self-esteem and their vision of how they can contribute to the world.

I can see that you are really upset and frustrated about this. You have such a strong sense of social justice and what is right and wrong. I love this for many reasons. You are right that it is not fair. Remember we spoke about how there are some things we can change and some things we can't? Here is the list of reasons why we can't change this one. You are such a good person. I can't wait to see how you use this passion in the future to change the world. Who do you think makes the most change in the world, human rights lawyers, activists, environmentalists or politicians?

Make sure they see, hear and learn about other autistic people

Education should be a window and a mirror. Children need to see around them accomplished and successful people just like them, who they can admire and aspire to be like. People who encourage them to pursue their dreams (the window). But children also need to see their 'ordinary' selves reflected back to them, in what they learn in school, on posters on the sides of buses, in books and what they see online, on the TV and in movies (the mirror).

You can tell your child every day about all the successful and fabulous autistic people out there (and how common autism is in general), but if they are not actually seeing these people around them it's all just words. Unfortunately, autism representation is hard to come by and this is going to take a bit of effort on your part. However, it should also be said that this is not purely an autistic issue, and affects other minority and disability groups, women and people of colour. You only need to think back to your own history classes to remember how white, able-bodied, western and male the focus was.

THE WINDOW

One of the famous autistic people who make my clients' eyes light up when I tell them they are autistic include Satoshi Tajiri (the creator of Pokémon), who as an added bonus helps bust the myths that autistic people have no imagination. It also shows how successful autistic people can be when allowed to follow their passions.

Greta Thunberg, climate activist (also a teenager who identifies herself as having Asperger's), is a perfect example of so many of the wonderful traits that can come along with autism: caring about the world, a keen eye for injustice and artifice, determination and outside-the-box thinking. Greta herself describes how Asperger's has been the gift that has helped her in her mission to literally save the world, and she is a fantastic role model for all autistic children. In the context of this book, Greta is particularly helpful because of how she embraces the strengths of her diagnosis and talks so openly about it.

The book *Different Like Me: My Book of Autism Heroes* by Jennifer Elder (Jessica Kingsley Publishers) has lots of examples of famous people (like Albert Einstein, Andy Warhol and Hans Christian Andersen) who have made our world a better and more interesting place.

Successful autistic people on YouTube:

- TedTalk: *How Autism Freed Me to Be Myself* by Rosie King

- TedTalk: *My Inner Life with Asperger's* by Alix Generous

- *Jake: Math Prodigy Proud of His Autism*, CBS News (although an exceptional case, this is also a lovely example of how focusing on interests and strengths is so beneficial).

Successful autistic authors:

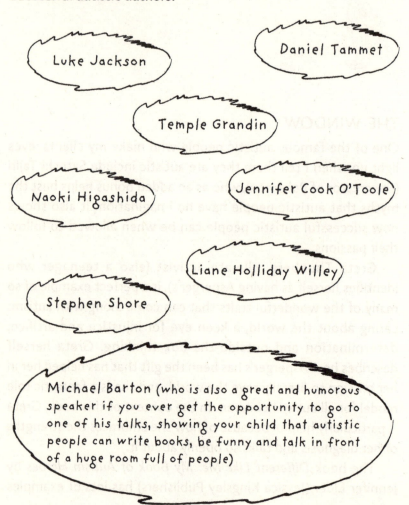

Luke Jackson

Daniel Tammet

Temple Grandin

Naoki Higashida

Jennifer Cook O'Toole

Liane Holliday Willey

Stephen Shore

Michael Barton (who is also a great and humorous speaker if you ever get the opportunity to go to one of his talks, showing your child that autistic people can write books, be funny and talk in front of a huge room full of people)

Teenage autistic actor Talia Grant has recently joined the UK TV show *Hollyoaks*, making her the first (of many I am sure) openly autistic adults to star in a mainstream drama. Other successful actors who are autistic include Dan Aykroyd, Daryl Hannah and Anthony Hopkins. In the UK, TV presenter Chris Packham has spoken openly about his late diagnosis and presented the excellent documentary *Asperger's and Me*. Also in the UK, Anne Hegarty (a television quiz personality) was a much-loved contestant and won 2018's *I'm a Celebrity Get Me Out of Here*.

THE MIRROR

Alongside all these fabulous, successful autistic people, also show your child normal, 'ordinary' autistic people just like them, because children also need to learn that they do not have to be a famous footballer or a maths genius to have value. Bring them to events with other autistic children. Try out some clubs. Arrange play dates. Include in this a broad diversity of disabled and different people.

TV programmes for younger children that include autistic characters include *Sesame Street* (Julia is a new autistic character) and *Pablo* (a children's cartoon created with autistic collaboration and who use autistic writers and actors).

TV programmes for older children and teenagers include *Atypical*, *The A Word* and *The Good Doctor* (although it should be noted that there are aspects to these that the autistic community find problematic). For general diversity, *Speechless* is a great TV programme with an actor with cerebral palsy in one of the leading roles.

For older teenagers, *The Drummer and The Keeper* is a moving and sweet movie about the friendship between two teenagers, one with bipolar disorder and one with Asperger's (although the actor playing this role is not himself autistic).

Recommended fictional books with autistic characters (as opposed to 'books *about* autism') include:

- *M is for Autism* by The Students of Limpsfield Grange School and Vicky Martin (Jessica Kingsley Publishers)

- *M in the Middle* by The Students of Limpsfield Grange School and Vicky Martin (Jessica Kingsley Publishers)

- *The London Eye Mystery* by Siobhan Dowd (Puffin)

- *Blue Bottle Mystery: An Asperger Adventure* by Kathy Hoopmann (Jessica Kingsley Publishers)

- *The Curious Incident of the Dog in the Night-Time* by Mark Haddon (Vintage)

- *A Boy Called Bat* by Elena K. Arnold (Waldon Pound Press) – and the rest of the series

- *Underdogs* by Chris Bonnello (Unbound Publishing).

Use books and videos

A lot of parents find that the structure of sitting down with a book, or watching a short video, is a good way to get their child's attention and takes the pressure off face to face conversations. Books can be used as a platform for further questions, such as 'Do you see any similarities between you and that boy?' or 'You feel a bit like that sometimes, don't you?'

Lots of parents have found it helpful (and less pressure on the child) to just leave positive autism-related books lying around the house. *I Am an Aspiengirl* by Tania Marshall (Aspiengirl publishers) is a great one for girls because of its large colour photographs and its positive, strengths-based focus. Doing this can lead to conversations arising in more natural ways and at your child's own pace, although many children have told me (with a smile on their face) that they were well aware of their parents' ploy.

Although it can sometimes be hard to find the right book for your child's age, language skills and how their autism presents, here is a selection of books explaining autism which parents I know have found helpful and autistic children have liked:

- *Benny Doesn't like to be Hugged* by Zeta Elliott and illustrated by Purple Wong (CreateSpace Independent Publishing Platform)

- *We're Amazing 1,2,3! A Story about Friendship and Autism (Sesame Street)* by Leslie Kimmelman (Golden Books)

- *Noah Chases the Wind* by Michelle Worthington and illustrated by Joseph Cowman (RedLeaf Press)

- *The Girl Who Thought in Pictures: The Story of Dr Temple Grandin* by Julia Finley Mosca and illustrated by Daniel Rieley (The Innovation Press)

- *Isaak and His Amazing Asperger Superpowers!* by Melanie Walsh (Walker Books)

- *My Autism Book: A Child's Guide to Their Autism Spectrum Diagnosis* by Glòria Durà-Vilà and Tamar Levi (Jessica Kingsley Publishers)

- *Say Hello to Me: A Story about a Little Girl on the Autism Spectrum* by April Charisse (AuthorHouse)

- *A Girl Like Tilly: Growing Up with Autism* by Helen Bates and illustrated by Ellen Li (Jessica Kingsley Publishers)

- *I am Aspiengirl: The Unique Characteristics, Traits and Gifts of Females on the Autism Spectrum* by Tania Marshall (Aspiengirl)

- *All My Stripes: A Story for Children with Autism* by Shania Rudolph and Danielle Royer, illustrated by Jennifer Zivoin (Magination Press)

- *Why Johnny Doesn't Flap: NT is OK!* by Clay Morton and Gail Morton, illustrated by Alex Merry (Jessica Kingsley Publishers)

- *The Superhero Brain: Explaining Autism to Empower Kids* by Christel Land (CreateSpace)

- *Freaks, Geeks and Asperger Syndrome: A User Guide to Adolescence* by Luke Jackson (Jessica Kingsley Publishers)

- *Dude, I'm an Aspie!* Kids Edition by Matt Friedman (lulu.com)

- *The Reason I Jump: The Inner Voice of a Thirteen-Year-Old Boy with Autism* by Naoki Higashida (Sceptre)

- *Fall Down Seven Times, Get Up Eight* by Naoki Higashida (Sceptre).

A few YouTube videos explaining autism you could try:

- *Amazing Things Happen* by Amazing Things Happen

- *Welcome to the Autistic Community* produced by the Autistic Self Advocacy Network

- *Explaining Autism to Children: ASD and Me* by Teresa De Mars

- *Shutting Down the Bullsh*t about Autism 2* (for older teenagers and parents who don't mind the language and content. Watch first yourself!).

For older children and teenagers I also highly recommend watching the Channel 4 documentary *Are You Autistic?* which approaches autism in a very positive, pro-neurodiversity way.

Write out your own personalised explanation

If none of those books or videos are quite right for your child, try writing something for them that is personalised instead. This can be in the format of a Social Story™ (a very specific format created by Carol Gray) but does not need to be. Search online for 'social stories explaining autism' to see different ideas which you can then adapt. Or adapt some of the phrases from this book. Remember it does not need to be perfect! Once it is positive about your child, positive about autism and in general has a kind and reassuring tone you are doing just fine.

Here are two examples of the kinds of things you could write that would be helpful for your child (depending on their age and language skills) (if you want to add some pictures or photos, even better):

Everyone is different.

People look different on the outside.

Daddy has blonde hair. Mummy and Ben have red hair.

Daddy is tall. Mummy is smaller.

Ben is the smallest but might be bigger than Daddy when he is grown up!

People are also different on the inside.

Mummy loves chocolate. Daddy loves lemonade. Ben loves ice cream.

Mummy loves reading. Ben and Daddy love movies.

Mummy is not a fast runner, even when she tries really hard!

Ben runs really fast. Much faster than Mummy!

Ben and Daddy love trains.

Ben and Daddy feel happy when they talk about trains.

Ben and Daddy don't like loud noises.

Ben and Daddy are autistic.

Mummy and Daddy and Ben all love each other.

Mummy and Daddy and Ben are a family.

Dear Melissa,

I know you read the words 'autism spectrum disorder' on a letter you saw on the kitchen table this morning with your name on it. The word disorder is unfortunate because it implies that there is something wrong with autism. But there isn't! A much better word to describe autism is 'condition' because autism really just means that your brain is wired a bit differently. It also means that people who are not autistic (sometimes called neurotypical people) sometimes don't understand things you do or say, and you don't understand things that they do or say. But in most ways autistic people and neurotypical people are just the same. We're all human!

Because you are autistic, you take in information from the world in a different way to neurotypical people. This can sometimes mean that you get overwhelmed in loud, crowded places. But there are lots of ways to help with this that we can talk about another day.

Autism is not an intellectual disability or a mental illness. It is a difference in your brain which started when you were growing in your mother's womb. This difference in your brain's 'wiring' has allowed you to develop all those amazing skills you have in maths, art and science. It is because of autism that you get such intense pleasure from learning and talking about planets. Being autistic means that you are a bit different to most people, but in so many good ways. It means that you are honest and brave and care about the world around you.

We love you and are so proud of you.

Mum and Dad

Try some creative, visual activities

All of these activities should be done in a light-hearted and fun way. If your child resists an activity, try to come at it from a different angle (e.g. more pictures, less writing). Or leave it and come back to it a different time. All of these activities emphasise how autism is just *one* part of all the many things that make your child wonderful.

Draw pictures (or glue photos) of different family members and friends, one person per page. Write words or draw pictures around them to represent things specific to that person, for example, loves books, loves bugs, strong, fast, hates peas, strong-willed, sometimes angry, sometimes silly, loves cuddles. Include 'autistic' as one of your child's words (and for any other person who is also autistic).

1. Psychologist and author Raelene Dundon, in her book *Talking with Your Child about Their Autism Diagnosis: A Guide for Parents* (Jessica Kingsley Publishers), uses the concept of 'ingredients' to talk about these individual differences, which is a nice, child-friendly way to come at it.

2. Encourage your child to write a poem, song or essay all about themselves, their strengths and challenges. Use this as a basis to talk about these things and make links to how they fit into the pattern of strengths and challenges in autism.

3. For younger children, or those with less language, create a 'folder' of pictures with no words. Include pictures of your child doing the things they love, and pictures of them with their family, friends and pets. Also include them doing something they don't particularly like, for example showing disgust at eating peas. You could then (for example) include a photo of them flapping. Go through the photos together, point to them individually and say things like 'James happy. James swimming. We love James. James flapping...autism. James doesn't like peas. James loves Mittens.'

Question 13: My child has very few words and I am really unsure of how much he understands. Do I need to tell him? How would I go about it?

SHORT ANSWER

You may not need to 'talk' that much about it with him yet. If you do, keep your language simple and concrete and also use pictures. But more than that, show him in your actions that you are positive and accepting towards his autism.

LONGER ANSWER

If you follow the positive, calm ways to talk about autism outlined in this book, it wouldn't hurt to try to explain autism to your child. If you do decide to do it, use mostly visuals (photos, pictures and videos) and keep your language very simple. There is an activity on page 79 designed for children with delayed language and cognitive skills which you can use and adapt just for him.

Even if he doesn't understand what you are trying to teach him, he will benefit from growing up in an accepting and understanding environment. With children with no verbal language, you can do things with them and approach them in a way that communicates a positive and accepting attitude towards autism, in your deeds more than your words (which they may not understand).

So even if you try some activities with photos and you feel that your child didn't take it in, my advice is to continue to talk positively about autism and difference around him assuming that he can understand. This will not only help him, but also his brothers, sisters and wider family members and community.

In general, parents and other adults need to learn to adapt their communication style and use a more concrete, autism-friendly style when communicating with autistic people who are non-verbal or developmentally delayed.

CHAPTER 5

What about Telling Other People?

Q&A TARA, AGED 9

1. What age were you when you found out about your autism diagnosis?

I was eight.

2. How did you find out?

Mummy told me when we were alone. We were in the car waiting for a sports match to finish.

3. How did you feel about it when you did find out?

I think I was excited. We watched a video on YouTube about autism.

4. Have your feelings about having autism changed since then?

Yes. I'm very negative about it, not as excited as I was. Now I know what it means, I feel that other people don't. I tell my friends I have it and they don't understand.

5. Did you know that you were different in some way before you were told about being autistic?

Yes, I did. I knew I was smarter and I didn't think like my friends.

6. What advice would you give parents about telling their child about their autism diagnosis?

Just tell them. In the car, it was just me and Mummy. We talked about the good things and how I was different to my cousin.

7. Have you read any books about autism that you think explain autism well?

No. We watched videos. My cousin has it too so I knew a little bit about it. I also know I'm not like him – I can talk, he can't.

8. In what ways has knowing about your autism diagnosis helped you (if any)?

I get help at school. I go into a social group and an enrichment group. I am making more friends now, that's good.

Question 14: I don't mind telling her she is autistic, but I worry about how she is going to be treated by other people (classmates, teachers, wider family and neighbours) when they find out

SHORT ANSWER

Be an autism ally. Educate people about autism. Help build autism-friendly communities.

LONGER ANSWER

You're right, your child learning to understand, accept and embrace her autism is just the first step. Her future wellbeing and happiness will also be dependent on how she is treated by the people around her in her schools, clubs and wider communities.

At home, you might help your child understand that, while she might not be great at languages and looking people in the eye, she is amazing at building things and has a glittering career ahead of her as an engineer. However, all of this career advice will come to nothing if she is in an education system that insists on her being successful in several subjects and she doesn't get past the first round of interviews for a job she is overqualified for because the company has no autism awareness.

In schools, it is my personal experience that, when handled correctly by the teacher, neurotypical classmates can actually be kinder and more accepting after being told about a child's autism diagnosis (even to those children who have previously been ostracised or bullied). In general, children sense difference and can be confused about it, leading to them either avoiding it or giving it negative attention. But being given a name and an explanation for a child's difference helps square the confusion away for children, and they can become kinder and more accepting as a result. These neurotypical children often say things like 'Oh I thought John was really weird, but now I know he just has autism', which is interesting in that it mirrors what autistic adults often say about themselves post diagnosis.

There is very interesting new research to suggest that the 'social issues' commonly associated with autism are actually down to neurotypical people, not autistic people. This research indicates that neurotypical people decide within moments (i.e. before the autistic person even starts speaking) that autistic people are less desirable to communicate with than neurotypical people and stop engaging with them. No wonder so many autistic people work so hard at masking their differences! This has been termed the 'double empathy problem' by autistic scholar Damian Milton, who argues quite convincingly that these 'issues' of communication and social encounters are a two-way thing.

We all clearly have a lot of work to do around becoming more empathic and accepting of difference, and autistic people need us to join their voices in agitating for change. Think about your local community (the restaurants, parks, sports clubs, shopping centres, schools) and ask yourself: What doesn't work for my child? Who needs to know more? What would I like to see changed? Engage with these people and services and educate them about what autism is. Help them move beyond the stereotypes.

For the purpose of developing autism-friendly communities, the Irish autism-led charity As I Am (www.asiam.ie) has produced industry-specific guidebooks (including for example, retail, restaurants and sports clubs) detailing ideas for how individual groups and services can become more autism friendly.

Tip

Get someone (it could be you, your child, an autistic advocate or a professional) to talk to your child's school about autism. In Ireland, Adam Harris, founder and CEO of As I Am, does this very well. Educate the children in the school about what autism is and it isn't. Help them understand why autistic people might flap or need movement breaks. Enlist their help for how they can create an autism-friendly class and school. In my experience, this kind of approach leads to significantly better and more accepting school experiences for autistic children.

Question 15: How will I tell her brothers and sisters?

SHORT ANSWER

This one is going to be brief because, actually, all the information you need is already in this book. Reread the book looking at all of the sample scripts and descriptions of autism. All of these can be used to describe autism to siblings, sometimes with just a little bit of tweaking. The activities involving pictures and photos can also be used to look at autism within the family context and to explain it to younger siblings. All of the advice about speaking openly, positively and realistically about autism still applies.

For brothers and sisters who are struggling for various reasons (for example, if they are being hurt by their autistic sibling, or on the receiving end of bullying because of them), before jumping into positivity and acceptance, it is first important to acknowledge their negative feelings. This ensures that they feel heard and understood, and so will help them be more open for further messages of acceptance. So for example you might say *'I understand how hurt and angry you feel when Jessica pulls your hair, you are right that she shouldn't do that. She doesn't yet understand why she shouldn't do it, but me and your mummy are working hard to try to teach her.'* Or *'I know you feel embarrassed in front of your friends when Jacob flaps and makes loud noises. I know you wish that as a family that we would all act "normal" all of the time. It's hard when people stare, I feel it too. But flapping and making noises is a part of who Jacob is, it is a part of his autism and he needs to do it to feel calm and happy. It would be like us telling you not to play football with your friends.'*

If there are autism siblings groups in your area I would recommend them, as they are great spaces for siblings to come together to offload and have fun with people who understand them.

One important piece of advice (which I have learned from autistic children is very important to them), is if you can and it is age appropriate, do tell your autistic child first about their diagnosis before their siblings.

CHAPTER 6

I Hear You but I'm Still Feeling Sad and Overwhelmed

Q&A ANDREW, AGED 13

1. What age were you when you found out about your autism diagnosis?

Eight or nine, I think, but I think I knew that I had some sort of diagnosis when I was eight and understood autism when I was nine.

2. How did you find out?

Pretty sure my parents just told me; it didn't mean that much at the time, though. I didn't really know what autism was then, and how much it would impact my life.

3. How did you feel about it when you did find out?

It didn't really impact me because I didn't know what it meant. I suppose I wouldn't really have cared at that stage.

4. Have your feelings about having autism changed over the years?

Yes, when I was really young I didn't think much of it. I gradually learned what it really meant. I used to think sometimes it made me unique but now I just think it sucks and destroys my life.

5. Did you know that you were different in some way before you were told about being autistic?

I suppose so, I couldn't really make friends and talk to people. Not different but I knew there were aspects to me that were different. I don't really know how to phrase it and I'm feeling negative about it at the moment.

6. What advice would you give parents about telling their child about their autism diagnosis?

It really depends what age. If they are nine onwards I might be a bit more cautious about it but it depends on whether they know they are different already. I don't think they would care so much before that age, I didn't at least. It might be better to have a reason for feeling different. It's certainly better to tell them that everyone's autism is different (when you've met one person with autism, you've met ONE person with autism). Tell them as soon as possible.

7. Have you read any books about autism that you think explain autism well?

I've read some phrases from books which half the time help but half the time are corny. But a book I would recommend, since it is nice and short, is *Hey Dude, I'm an Aspie*. Also, as a film recommendation, I do recommend *The Drummer and The Keeper* as it is also very entertaining.

8. How do you feel about having more than one diagnosis?

For me personally, sometimes I find it hard to deal with. At one moment I think about autism, then about dyspraxia, and then about dysgraphia, and then all the other problems I have. As to me it seems I can't have a social life, do my work in school as well as I would like to, and I can't play sports which to me seems to be very important in this world.

9. In what ways has knowing about your autism diagnosis helped you (if any)?

It is much better knowing as you can tell people why you may act a certain way and you can understand it more clearly yourself. It certainly does help to know there is a reason but at the same time, I just wish I simply didn't have autism and that happens a lot. But in the end, it is certainly better knowing.

I'm sorry if some of this is depressing but I do hope that this is helpful. My father is quite obviously on the spectrum but does not have a diagnosis, and I do think his life may have been easier if he did.

Question 16: OK, I hear you. I agree that it's probably a good idea to tell him he is autistic, and I know that I need to be positive about it, but I'm not feeling a bit positive about it. I'm feeling angry and sad and I wish my child wasn't born autistic. What do I do now?

SHORT ANSWER

Be kind to yourself and take some time to grieve. If you need extra help, ask for it. If all else fails, fake it till you make it.

LONGER ANSWER

This book strongly embraces and celebrates difference and neurodiversity, and these are things that I believe in and care about. However, here are some things that are also true. Autism is hard. It is hard to have, and it is hard to parent. Seeing your child suffering because no one in their class will play with them is hard. Supporting your child through associated medical difficulties like seizures is hard. Seeing your child having meltdowns and not being able to understand or help is hard. Worrying about how your child is going to survive in a world that doesn't understand them is hard. Seeing your extremely bright child failing in every subject in school is hard. Knowing that your child is never going to speak or live independently is hard. Fighting for services, managing appointments, sitting on lengthy waiting lists and dealing with professionals telling you how you should and shouldn't parent your own child is hard. Worrying about what advice to follow, what therapy to choose, will you be able to afford it, all of this is hard. Even though you've been told many times it is not your fault, worrying that your child has autism because of something you did, or something you could have avoided, is hard. It is important that these realities are not forgotten in the autism narrative. As one autistic young adult said to me, 'I really don't care what we call autism, or what other people think of me. I just want a job and not to live with my parents forever.'

'I wish I never had autism' is something I hear a lot from older autistic children and teenagers; thankfully much less so from autistic adults who, with the benefit of age, maturity and hindsight, have learned to accept and embrace their differences.

'I wish my child didn't have autism' is something that many parents have thought, and some have shared online on social media and blogs. Because of the public nature of these posts, they have of course been read by many autistic people, who have spoken about how exceptionally hurtful these comments are to them.

Being autistic is who I am. So, if you're saying you are sorry that I have that, you're saying that you are sorry that I exist. And if I weren't autistic, I wouldn't be me. (John, 24)

On a related note, the autistic community is particularly upset about parents of autistic children writing memoirs and uploading videos online which can detail publicly the very intimate, distressing and private details of autistic children's lives without their consent. They make the point that, as well as being a breach of privacy and consent, these parents are opening their children up to potential humiliation, as future carers, partners or employers are privy to very personal aspects of their lives.

It is very important that to your child you make clear the distinction between wanting to take away any pain from their life, and wanting them to be a completely different person (which is what they hear when they hear you wish they had not been born with autism). Like all children, autistic children need to hear that they are wonderful and unique and special, and that you love them for all that they are, even the difficult parts.

However, this does not mean that you can or should not grieve, which is in fact a very normal reaction around the time of a diagnosis, even when you were expecting it. Allow yourself to grieve. Be kind to yourself. Cry. Sit with and acknowledge those feelings of anger, sorrow, blame and denial (you will have to deal with them at some stage). Talk to your friends or partner. Meditate. Talk to a therapist. Talk to other parents of autistic children. Join a support group. Take some time off work if you can. Exercise.

All of these things will help you come to a place of acceptance around the autism diagnosis, a place when you can talk openly to your child about autism in all the calm, positive ways you have read about in this book.

If the time has come when your child needs to know about their diagnosis and you are still not in the right place, I'm afraid you're going to have to fake it till you make it. I think you might surprise yourself in a few years at having come to accept something you never felt you would, and autism becomes the new 'normal'.

Question 17: I'm feeling really overwhelmed by all of this. Just tell me one thing I can do right now

SHORT ANSWER

Start listening to autistic people.

LONGER ANSWER

Autistic people are going to teach you more about autism than I ever can. Choose one way to listen to them that suits you best. Your options include going to a talk, buying a book, reading some tweets, reading a blog or watching a YouTube video. Listen to their struggles and successes because it will help you better understand autism and your child. It will also give you the confidence and the language to be able to talk to your child about autism in positive and realistic ways.

Here are a few to start with:

1. Search online for this free information booklet (it is easily found): *Welcome to the Autistic Community* produced by the Autism Self Advocacy Network (all of whom are autistic).

2. Watch this video on YouTube: Rosie King's TedTalk: *How Autism Freed Me to Be Myself*.

3. Read this autobiography: *The Reason I Jump: The Inner Voice of a Thirteen-Year-Old Boy with Autism* by Naoki Higashida (Sceptre).

4. If you're on Twitter, search for the #ActuallyAutistic hashtag and start following some autistic advocates.

Q&A ADAM HARRIS, FOUNDER AND CEO OF ASIAM.IE, AGED 24

1. What age were you when you found out about your autism diagnosis?

I can't remember a time in which I didn't know that I was autistic. From a very young age my parents were asking questions and pursuing my diagnosis. I was in an autism early intervention class aged four and then in special education for a further two years. My parents were always very open in talking about autism with me in a positive, age-appropriate light.

As I grew up I learnt more and more about it and when I moved to mainstream my parents openly discussed it with teachers and other parents. Even my peer group were given a talk on difference and I would have no problem discussing my diagnosis. I guess as I entered the teenage years, though, I started to see it less as this cool 'superpower' and more as something which made people treat me differently. It was only in my late teen years that I changed my view again and began to see it as a positive if other people learnt to understand it.

2. How did you find out?

My parents would say things like 'You know how you are very good at history and know all the flags of the world but you don't like crowds and sometimes you can get very upset – that's called Asperger's.' I also was not going to have the wool pulled over my eyes – I would openly ask why I went to a different school, in a completely different town, to my brother and sister. I wanted to know why I was being taken to see so many professionals in different hospitals and clinics. As I got a little bit older, I was encouraged to watch programmes and read books about autism and this led to me being very proud of it and seeing it almost as a superpower.

3. How did you feel about it when you did find out?

Initially, it was just totally normal. Just like being told the colour of your eyes or the hand you write with. My parents were so open about it, at such a young age, it was second nature to me. As an older child, say between 8 and 11, I was very proud and thought it was a cool difference which associated me with so many interesting characters and famous people. However, as I got older, around the senior years in national school and entering puberty, I then began to resent the diagnosis because I saw it as the reason why many people treated me differently or set limits on my abilities. It was only as I reached the older teenage years that I decided it was society's view not my way of thinking which was at fault. That's why I started AsIAm.

4. Have your feelings about having autism changed over the years?

Definitely. I think they have been influenced by both the maturing of my own understanding of what it meant to be autistic starting in a very positive simple space, becoming frustrating as I grew older and saw the limitations and becoming positive as I grew to understand the positives. They have also been influenced by the attitudes of others; playing a role in changing those attitudes has also changed my own perception.

5. Did you know that you were different in some way before you were told about being autistic?

This is a difficult question because I was diagnosed at a young age but, yes, I feel I always knew that I was different and that is why I think it was important that my parents were open with me – I think I would've been twice as frustrated if I didn't understand the 'why'.

6. What advice would you give parents about telling their child about their autism diagnosis?

It doesn't need to be a really awkward 'birds and the bees' style conversation. The child's autism is totally normal to them – all you are doing is explaining how they already see the world. Do it in a casual, age appropriate way and let them lead with the questions!

7. Have you read any books about autism that you think explain autism well?

I think *The Reason I Jump* is magnificent and so accessible.

8. If you have more than one diagnosis, how do you feel/what do you think about having more than one diagnosis?

I think it is really important that people know that autistic people, like everyone, are 3-D. Our needs go beyond 'Ah well he is autistic'. This applies to other developmental diagnoses but also areas such as mental health and sexuality.

9. In what ways has knowing about your autism diagnosis helped you (if any)?

It has given me a reference point to understand myself and a shield to protect me from the unforgiving attitudes of others. Being autistic means I have to problem solve every day and so it has made me more self-aware than many other people, I would think.

In Summary

Question 1: What actually is autism anyway? People talk about it like I'm supposed to understand. I have tried reading about it online but it's all very confusing
There is no short answer to this one.

Question 2: What do I call it? Is it autism, autism spectrum disorder or Asperger's syndrome? What about PDD-NOS? Different professionals and parents on online forums seem to use different words for it
Call it autism. He is autistic. She is on the autism spectrum.

Question 3: What about all this 'autistic person' versus 'person with autism' stuff? What is the right way to say it?
At the moment, I use 'autistic person' because it is what most autistic people seem to prefer.

Question 4: Is he high or low functioning? Where on the autism scale does she fall?
There is no autism 'scale' and the terms high and low functioning (although often used by professionals) often end up being meaningless and stigmatising. Autism is a spectrum; everyone on it is different.

Question 5: But aren't we all a little bit autistic?
No.

Question 6: Do I really need to tell him he is autistic?
Yes, I think you do. Without a diagnosis your child is still autistic, just without the tools to understand or cope with it. He needs to understand himself. He needs to link in with other autistic people. Autistic people unanimously agree it's better to know. Not telling him may have a negative impact on his future mental health.

Question 7: I know he is autistic, but I don't want to tell him or other people. I don't want him to be labelled
Autism is not a label. It is an identity.

Question 8: My child has a few different diagnoses. Which ones do I tell her about? It seems too much to tell her about all of them
Personally, I think start with the one that affects her the most. Definitely at some point tell her about the autism, and add on the others over time only if needed or helpful.

Question 9: She works so hard at fitting in – won't a diagnosis make her feel different?
Yes, it will. But she is already different. Through knowing about her diagnosis, she can meet other autistic children who are different in the same way as she is. It will help her understand and embrace these differences. Her increased self-awareness and acceptance will most likely lead to better, truer friendships with both neurotypical and autistic people.

Question 10: Won't she start using autism as an excuse to get out of things that she doesn't like?
Yes, she might. However, it is more helpful to see autism as a possible reason for some of the things she finds difficult, rather than an excuse. Teach her to advocate for herself instead.

Question 11: When is the best time to tell him?
The earlier the better, but it's never too late.

Question 12: OK, I'm ready. Now how do I actually go about it? I don't have a clue what to do or say!

1. Start talking about neurodiversity.

2. Start talking about strengths.

3. Be the air steward you want to see.

4. Rethink autistic 'problems'.

5. Make sure they see, hear and learn about other autistic people.

6. Use books and videos.

7. Write out your own personalised explanation.

8. Try some creative, visual activities.

Question 13: My child has very few words and I am really unsure of how much he understands. Do I need to tell him? How would I go about it?
How about trying in case he does understand, but don't labour the point or expect too much? Keep your language simple and use pictures.

Question 14: I don't mind telling her she is autistic, but I worry about how she is going to be treated by other people (classmates, teachers, wider family and neighbours) when they find out
Be an autism ally. Educate people about autism. Help build autism-friendly communities.

Question 15: How will I tell her brothers and sisters?
All of the sample scripts, descriptions of autism and activities in this book can be used to describe autism to siblings, sometimes with a little tweaking. The advice about speaking openly and positively about autism and difference in general still applies;

however, remember to hear and acknowledge negative feelings as well. Siblings groups can be great if available. If possible, tell your autistic child first.

Question 16: OK, I hear you. I agree it's probably a good idea to tell him he is autistic, and I know I need to be positive about it, but I'm not feeling a bit positive about it. I'm feeling angry and sad and I wish my child wasn't born autistic. What do I do now? Be kind to yourself and take some time to grieve. If you need extra help, ask for it. If all else fails, fake it till you make it.

Question 17: I'm feeling really overwhelmed by all of this. Just tell me one thing I can do right now Start listening to autistic people.

Index

Also by Davida Hartman

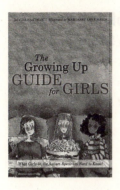

The Growing Up Guide for Girls
What Girls on the Autism Spectrum Need to Know!
Davida Hartman
Illustrated by Margaret Anne Suggs

72 pages
Hardback
ISBN: 978 1 84905 574 1

The Growing Up Guide for Girls is a one-stop guide for young girls on the autism spectrum explaining all they need to know about puberty and adolescence.

The pre-teen and teenage years are a bumpy time when bodies change, emotions are high and peers are developing at different paces. Using simple, literal language and delightful colour illustrations, this book explains the facts about body changes such as growing hair in new places, periods, wearing a bra and keeping spots away! It gives cool tips on what makes a real friend, what it means to have a crush on somebody and how to stay safe online. Most importantly, it explains that every body is beautiful and unique and encourages young girls with autism to celebrate difference! Perfect preparation for the teenage years for girls aged 9–14.

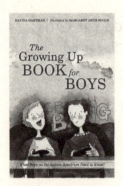

The Growing Up Book for Boys

What Boys on the Autism Spectrum Need to Know!

Davida Hartman

Illustrated by Margaret Anne Suggs

68 pages
Hardback
ISBN: 978 1 84905 575 8

The Growing Up Book for Boys explains the facts behind the growth spurts, body changes and mood swings of adolescence for boys aged 9–14 on the autism spectrum.

The pre-teen and teenage years are a confusing time when bodies start acting with a will of their own, friendships change and crushes start to develop. Using direct, literal language and cool colour illustrations, this book tells boys all they need to know about growing hair in new places, shaving, wet dreams and unexpected erections. It's full of great advice on what makes a real friend, how to keep spots away and how to stay safe online. Most importantly, it explains that every body is amazing and unique and encourages young boys with autism to celebrate difference!

Beating Anxiety
What Young People on the Autism Spectrum Need to Know
Davida Hartman
Illustrated by Kate Brangan

112 pages
Paperback
ISBN: 978 1 78592 075 2

Many young people on the autism spectrum struggle with anxiety, but did you know there are lots of simple things you can do to tackle it?

This illustrated book will help you to identify what makes you anxious and contains heaps of activities to calm your body and mind, stop unhealthy anxiety building up and head off anxious feelings in the future. Did you know that giving your anxiety a silly name (like Dr Dread!) will give you power over it? That pretending you are a jellyfish can make your body feel better? That writing your worries down and jumping on them as hard as you can will help to squash them?

Ideal for children and young people aged 8–14, the ideas in this book will help you feel less stressed at home, at school and with friends, and give you healthy habits and coping techniques to last a lifetime.